Silicon Valley Survival Guide:

4 Steps to Living Your Dream Life in Silicon Valley

By John Frye

Table of Contents

Preface

Introduction

Step 4: Building A Reputation

Conclusion

Preface

Hi there! My name is John Frye and I am a 19 year old entrepreneur in Silicon Valley. I have had some pretty terrible failures and pretty fantastic successes ever since I moved to California when I was 17 from Florida.

I started attending UC Santa Cruz and started a business buying old cars from a police auction, fixing them up a bit and selling them at a higher price. While still flipping cars I moved to San Jose and attended De Anza College to save money. After a while in San Jose all my cars broke and I had made no friends in my new city or school and fell into a depression. I took a part time job as a doorman at a bar to earn extra cash which meant I would get home many nights at 4 a.m. after hanging around people I had nothing in common with. I would lull out of bed at noon everyday, so mad that I did not have the energy to get up any sooner. I started doubting myself, I would cry into my pillow when I got home and be so mad I wasn't building a startup like I dreamed of back in Florida.

I felt like a lost and alone failure.

I decided at the advice of my closest friends and family to put my dreams of making it in Silicon Valley on hold and moving back to Florida to put my life back together. I called my dad and booked the plane ticket back to Florida to start over. That day seemed to slowly play out without me even noticing. I was so afraid of my depression that I just wanted to feel comfortable again, not even thinking about my dreams I had been looking forward to since I was 13.

Then a miracle happened.

Earlier that year, still full of hope and energy, I had applied to go to an entrepreneurial bootcamp in the heart of Silicon Valley to help launch an app idea I had. I had made it pretty far in the interview process and had lots of hope that I would get in, but they had not gotten back to me in over a month so I just assumed I didn't make the cut. Then after studying one night I got a call, I remember the feelings so vividly it could have happened just now. It was about 7 at night when I got the call so I was a bit perplexed as to who it might be. I checked the phone and it was a number I did not recognize, I went ahead and pressed the answer button.

"Hello"- Me

"Hi, is this John Frye?"- Caller

"Yes, how can I help you?"- Me

"I am calling about Draper University…"- Caller

"Oh! Yes I have not heard from you in a while!"- Me

"Really? I did not know that my apologies, well My name is X and I have some news for you John."- Caller

"Ok…"- John

"Congrats! You've made it into the program and you have also made it on the show Startup U, it will be on ABC Family!"- Caller

It was if someone had just drained out all the feeling of my body, I could not feel the phone in my hand, clothes on my body or my lungs breathing. I was in utter shock. I just stood there for what felt like a century and stared out in the distance blankly, then all of the sudden the feeling washed back into me, a hot wave of pure joy cascaded over me.

"Really?!?!"- Me

"Yes, yes! You just have to promise not to tell anyone, here is what you will do next…….."- Caller

It was an absolute miracle, I remember being in such a dazed state of joy I couldn't even cry, my mind just couldn't process this information fully. I immediately called my dad and told him everything, the spark that had left me had been ignited once again.

I went through the program, the show aired and I started my first real startup and continue to run it today. I have learned a lot about how to survive in Silicon Valley and how to make it through when times get tough. I will teach you through 4 quick chapters how to start living your dream life in Silicon Valley!

Intro

So, you have heard the tales of all the Silicon Valley legends who have become billionaires and lead the most badass lives.

Steve Jobs, Elon Musk, Bill Gates, Mark Zuckerberg and Evan Spiegel are names you often heard about in the media and in the movies. They (mostly) have humble beginnings and through the magic of the tech industry have managed to create world changing companies that have touched billions of people's lives for the better and made billions in the process.

But what about the rest of us?

What if you were not born out of the womb furiously typing away in Objective C, the iOS language, creating the next billion dollar idea? What if you have never done anything "techy" beyond using Google to do a report on the high accidental death rates of cows in Switzerland? Most people are not a math wiz, marketing ninja or crazy coding machine, they are just everyday people. But, there are all kinds of people who have figured out how to make life amazing and still live the "Silicon Valley Dream".

Here's how you figure it out.

Chapter 1
Find Your Talent

One thing that you absolutely must have is a talent and by that I mean a specific skill that you can use to add value to anything you work on. Look at the skills you already have, you may just be able to apply something you already do to make it in Silicon Valley.

Here is a list of very valuable skills:
- Programming
  - Back End
  - Front End
  - Degree in Computer Science
  - iOS/ Android or Web
- Graphic Artist (UI/UX Engineer)
  - Adobe, Prototyping Software (Sketch, Invision etc.)
- Sales
- Customer Relations
- Hardware/ Mechanical Engineer

- Logistics Engineer

These are a few examples of skills that you probably you could use to easily transition and get a job, start a company or join a founding team. However, if you don't have any of these skills that is totally fine. You can develop skills on top of natural talents and use certain methods to quickly acquire them.

Here are some natural talents or traits with corresponding skills:

Trait: Logical

If you're the person who values reason above all else, loves data and was good at things like math and science in school then programming might be for you.

Skill: Programming (Back End)

If you really love numbers, structure and using reason then back end coding might be a great path for you. If a program is a car then the engine would be the back end. It is the thing that is constantly making everything happen and is pretty complicated while being concealed to the user.

Learning Method: Coding Bootcamp

There are many "bootcamps" that will teach you how to code in a few weeks or months by completely immersing you in the learning process and having you create real programs. Most bootcamps don't focus specifically on back end but here are a couple that do.

- The Iron Yard
  - Iron Yard has over 25 locations and a larger network than most coding bootcamps.
- General Assembly
  - They offer classes on just about any skill you would need in Silicon Valley, the one linked is specifically for back end coding.
- AppAcademy

- This is a very high quality and selective program as they don't charge you upfront. They take a percentage of your income when you get a job (they do have a $5,000 deposit they give back once the program is over).

Now I know you might say "I can't spend thousands of dollars on this, that's ludicrous!!!". Well hold your horses because this is not *spending* money, it's *investing* money to have a greater return later. You may spend a few thousand, maybe you even go into a bit of debt but getting a job starting around $60,000-$120,000 means it will literally repay itself in months. With that in mind I will recommend more programs that might seem expensive but have an amazing return on investment (ROI), use your discretion of course but be willing to invest in yourself to reap the rewards.

Learning Method: Online School

If you have always been good at sticking to online courses and doing side projects this might be a better route for you to take. There are many places online where you can learn how to code and over a few months or a year without having to quit your job.

- Udemy
    - They have free and paid courses with 18,000+ instructors, one of the most popular online course sites.
- Khan Academy
    - Khan Academy offers free course in most academic subjects and have a very interactive learning platform.
- Codecademy
    - They focus solely on code and have built a platform that has over 25+ million users.

Being able to learn how to code is valuable enough in Silicon Valley because there is a major lack of software engineers. If you gain a specialty like backend programming that makes you <u>that</u>

much more valuable. Figure out what steps to take to gain this skill to check that off your to-do list.

Trait: Creative (Artistic)

You're the one who was painting, singing or doing crafts all through your childhood and everyone around you saw that you had a knack for it. There are many routes you can take with that but one in particular extremely valuable in Silicon Valley.

Skill: Designer (UI/UX Engineer)

First, let's go ahead and define what a "UI/UX Engineer" actually means. The acronyms stand for User Interface and User Experience, User Interface is the layout so all the buttons, words, banners and whatnot. User Experience is the "feel" of the design, is it sleek and modern? Robust and bold? Minimalist and simple?

So that is what a UI/UX Engineer is, keep the term and use it from now on so as not to confuse or get confused. Being a UI/UX Engineer you will help create the layout, function and feel of a product.

Learning Method: Developer Bootcamp (Front End)

Again, bootcamps are a great way to get started quickly and dive into your new career after only a few weeks or months of learning. Here are some more bootcamps:

- Bloc
  - This is specifically for front end designers!
- App Academy
  - I will suggest them again as I have heard the really good things about them and hear of them the most.
- Full Stack Academy
  - They focus on making you a well rounded developer, it is an on site program out of New York.

By the way, if you apply and get rejected to any of these there is an exhaustive list of all the developer bootcamps on skilledup.com under an article called "Ultimate Guide to Coding Bootcamps".

Learning Method: Online

They are the same as the last one I mentioned, here they are again.

- Udemy
    - They have free and paid courses with 18,000+ instructors, one of the most popular online course sites.
- Khan Academy
    - Khan Academy offers free course in most academic subjects and have a very interactive learning platform.
- Codecademy
    - They focus solely on code and have built a platform that has over 25+ million users.

Trait: Hustler

Where you selling your neighbors lemonade every since you could say "That will be a dollar please."? Have you always been willing to push the limits, stay up late, work hard and not quit till you made something happen? If you're a hustler you can definitely get some concrete skills to compliment your natural ability.

Skill: Business Development

Generally I hate using the phrase "business development" because it is such a broad and fluffy term but I want to wrap together a couple skills that all do one thing, make money. Marketing and getting customers is making money, selling is making money, creating partnerships is making money. For the purposes of this book we will call it business development, now here are a couple places you can learn it.

Learning Method: Startup Bootcamp

Similar to the programming bootcamp the startup bootcamp will teach you the fundamentals of the business side of running a startup. Here are some great programs to go to:

- Draper University
  - A 7 week program started by billionaire venture capitalist Tim Draper this program will teach you how to think like a silicon valley entrepreneur. I am actually an alumni of this program so I highly recommend it (tell them John Frye sent you).
- Hydra
  - Hydra is also a bootcamp where you learn the basics of starting a startup and how to be an effective silicon valley style entrepreneur.
- Uncollege
  - This is not an actual "bootcamp", it is more of a college placement program but is still very useful. This has less of an entrepreneurial focus but you will still learn a ton about real

world skills and how to apply them to a new or existing business.

Learning Method: Online School

- "How to Build a Startup" Course
    - This is a course made by a silicon valley legend Steve Blank. It will teach you the basics of how to build a startup but will also be very useful if you want to join a company.
- Stanford Courses
    - This is a series of courses that will give you well rounded knowledge on a variety of subjects.
- "Business Development for Startups" Course
    - Another Udemy course, not by a silicon valley legend but worth looking into, always helps to learn material from a different angle.

With these skills in hand you are much more likely to thrive in either creating your own startup or joining an existing company.

Going through that process will help you gain the skills you need to be successful in Silicon Valley if you don't already have them. After getting the skills you need a way of breaking into the network of people in order to get better access to the opportunities that are abundant.

Chapter 2
Building Your Network

So now you're skilled! What's next?!? Well, you have to create a way to easily gain access to opportunities, resources, mentors and more that you need to take the leap.

You are now going to start "networking" but not in the sleazy way, in the natural human way, by making relationships. Admittedly at times it can be really challenging to get people to like, trust or even listen to you. However, if you're willing to put in the work and time and be a genuine person you will be able to build a solid network. Luckily the internet has democratized networking and you can get your message across to most any notable person in the world. Also it is a scalable, quick and repeatable way to network and build relationships with people. The downside is it can be spammy, unprofessional and hurt your reputation if it is done incorrectly enough times. There are many legitimate ways of building a real, human connection with someone even if it's through a computer.

Online

There are many strategies of contacting people online thanks to tools like e-mail, facebook, snapchat, twitter, youtube and many other services that have become available recently.

Cold E-mail

This is a great way to get someone's attention if you ask me because it's literally going to the same inbox their business deals, employees and high net worth friends use to contact them. Before you start crafting the cold e-mail you are going to need their email address. I use an email permeator and a tool called rapportive to find an email address to someone I don't know. The email permeator spreadsheet can be by googling "e-mail permeator spreadsheet". Generally you can guess someone's email by simply putting their first name in front of their website domain. It would look like this:

name@theirwebsite.com

Once you have obtained the email there is a certain way you should go about doing the email. Many people just start gushing out how much they admire that person and start pitching why they need to be in contact with them and almost begging them for help. That is NOT an effective method for reaching out to people, would you read paragraphs of that if you were them?

There is an amazing tip that Tam Pham talks about in his book "How To Network", you actually *give* the person you're trying to contact something. You might wonder what you have to give to them, that's where you get creative. Here is an example, I love listening to podcasts about startups and entrepreneurs. There are some very high profile hosts of these podcasts that I would love to have a personal relationship with. Now, most of the entrepreneurs they interview are in their late 20's so that is most likely what their demographic of viewers is. I am not even 20, I am in generation Z which is the generation after millennial's which means I have insight on a new demographic. I can come up with a list of 10 things that any show host could do to try and capture more generation Z listeners once the millennial's start to run dry. That is something of major value and something I know intimately since I am not only a member of that generation, I study it. So come up with a list of 10 ways the recipient and do whatever they are doing better but keep it short and sweet, here is a template you can use.

Hey Recipient!

I love your X that you do, I've recently become a huge fan! I am also a Y, and I think I know some ways you can get more Y's to use X.

1. Reason #1
2. Reason #2
3. Reason #3
4. Reason #4

5. Reason #5
6. Reason #6
7. Reason #7
8. Reason #8
9. Reason #9
10. Reason #10

I really hope this helps, I am excited to keep using and sharing X. If you want to more about Y's I think I could dive deeper than the 10 above and hopefully give you more useful insight.

Thank,
Your Name

Short, simple and to the point. The best part is you didn't ask for anything and I promise this will at a minimum throw them off and little and could easily make them write back ready to have a coffee with YOU.

So you want to find two groups of people, one extremely high level and one medium level. Extremely high would be Mark Zuckerberg, medium would be the head of a department. Create a large list of high level (around 100) and a smaller list of medium level (20-40) because you will likely get much more of the medium level hence the smaller list.

Find these people by looking at some of your favorite companies, products, blogs or something similar and just take down the names in a list. Use the email permeator and rapportive to get the email and make their 10 improvements and send it off, let the relationships begin!

Twitter

This is great because you don't have to hunt to find their handle, you also will want to take a different approach when trying to get their attention. The biggest way to get noticed by someone big is to constantly engage with them. Now let me define engage, that is not "Please X follow me!!1!!1". Everybody hates that including the people who are just casual and fanatic fans of the person. Real engagement would be more like

"Wow, you're always so insightful. I'm ready to buy the new book!". Doing this on a consistent basis will get you noticed by that person. Even if they are a total asshole they know that their fans are the reason why they are big so they want to keep the people who are giving them support happy so they keep supporting.

Also making really cool or funny videos, pictures, songs etc. about them and tagging them in it. Again you have to get creative, think of them and think about how your talents could translate into an interesting post about them. Try it a few times and if they don't respond just move on to the next person on the list.

Snapchat

Many high profile people share their snapchat to show stories and make their snapchat handles public. If you get their snapchat and send them messages about how you love them or their work they may reply. You may not want give them help through snapchat but you can probably ask for some form of contact once you've built a bit of trust.

Facebook

Once you get some people who are in your network who you can add on facebook you'll notice you will start having mutual friends with lots of high level people. You can throw out a lot of friend requests and see who accepts. Once they do you can use one of the items on your list of 10 things that could help them. Remember, always try and give them something in the beginning, do not try to take. Also you may ask some of the mutual friends of the people who are high level to introduce you but be warned that can burn people and be very irritating so use this trick with caution.

LinkedIn

This is similar to the Facebook method, you can add high to medium level people you can mutual connections with and see what happens. I would again suggest doing a short version of the cold email with one of the 10 items on your list.

In Person: Local

Not everyone can hop on a plane to San Francisco at all let alone for something like networking. So you can utilize meeting people locally who are entrepreneurial, medium level people who might have connections to Silicon Valley or at least mutual connections.

Meetups

Meetups are the absolute #1 way to meet people and the best place to find meetups is meetup.com. Find a meetup related to your skill (designer, writer etc.) and attend that to meet people that share a skill. Also try meetups for people who are entrepreneurs or from Silicon Valley and say you are looking into moving to Silicon Valley.

When meeting with people and trying to network it all boils down to one thing: be nice. Just listen to them, be genuinely interested and engage and don't worry about collecting a card until when the event ends. Even better ask them if you can buy them a drink and keep chatting to foster the relationship further. After all that it is not unreasonable to ask for contact information, however make sure you still try and add value to them somehow.

In Person: Silicon Valley

Conferences
If you are lucky enough to have the chance to go out to Silicon Valley there is another level that is not in your home town most likely; conferences. Conferences are everywhere in the Bay Area for all kinds of reasons, so find ones that pertain to you and get tickets to go.

When you are meeting fellow attendees and find someone interesting you can follow the same guidelines from the local meetups. You probably want to meet the speakers though who will be the people on your list. These situations can be tricky depending on how big the speaker and event is.

If they have a Q&A try really hard to make sure you get a question in. Frame the question in a way that will transition well for if you see them later. Wait for them to get off the stage and try and be the first person to see them. Start to follow up on the question and lead into how you might be able to help. Tell them you thought of a few key things that might help them and ask if you can follow up on email.

Meetups

These are very valuable because you are much more likely to get connected with people who are will be able to help you transition into Silicon Valley both as friends and as references for getting a job. Go about this the same way as above, just be nice and be casual and focus on giving and making friends (not contacts).

Chapter 3
Getting In

Now you have a talent and network, what else can there be to do!? Well, you not living and working there yet. Using the tools you know have you can get the job and living situation that will be part of your new dream life in Silicon Valley!

<u>Getting the Job</u>

If you plan on getting a job then you can utilize all the resources you have created for yourself. However you have to connect all the pieces to make to make it work for you. You may already have a LinkedIn, if you do use it to sign up for Angel List. Angel List is like LinkedIn but for startups and much better designed then LinkedIn is. You will be able to see all your common connections to startups hiring in the area. Start looking at available jobs that you are eligible and seeing what common connections you have. Also look on the traditional platforms for tech jobs like craigslist and Indeed and manually check to see if you have any connections.

Once you have identified a couple of common connections at places where you would like to work start reaching out to them. Again, you want to try to helping them more then you are helping yourself. When you are asking them don't just blurt it out in the first sentence, that's like asking for sex before your first date. I would suggest set up a way to give them something, like a coffee, before making the ask. Here an example of a good conversation leading up to the ask:

"Hey Stephanie! How are you?" - Me

"I am great thanks! How are you John?" - Stephanie

"How are you liking working at Google?" - Me

"Great! I love it, so many free perks lolz" - Stephanie

"Haha, hey would you like to catch up more over coffee next Saturday @ 11am? My treat!"- Me

"Sure, see you then!"- Stephanie

Everything is teed up now, give her that awesome new gingerbread coffee she's been dying to try and ease into the ask. Make sure you have done your research and figure out the best way to add value.

"Hey so do you know what's new with the maps department?" - Me

"Yeah a bunch of their front end designers left to create a vitamin delivery startups, weird haha." - Stephanie

"Yeah that is weird haha, you know I actually graduated from App Academy and made a bunch of google maps re designs. Maybe I should apply, what do you think?" - Me

"Oh definitely! I'll totally vouch for you to the recruiters, by the way they really like to when you use the words 'my purpose' a lot. No idea why." - Stephanie

"Wow, awesome thanks so much!" - Me

Now, if you don't live a place where you get a coffee this whole conversation could be had over phone, skype or a messenger. Using this goldmine of information you can now apply much more confidently to get that job. Keep in mind this may take several tries to get it but it should make the process better and shorter if executed well.

Getting a Gig

There are more and more people hopping on the freelance band wagon so they can work from wherever, whenever. This approach is not for everyone, you have to have great self discipline and time management and be able to to work without people around you. If you are a focused and disciplined worker who strives on working solo then this might be a great path for you.

To get in networking also really helps with this, I would strongly recommend the strategy above for getting a full time job and applying it to getting a free lance job. Other than that here are the best platforms to look for freelance work.

- Upwork- Many of the freelancing sites recently merged to create one big platform that is Upwork.
- Angel List- Go to the job section and filter your search with "contract", good resource for startup jobs.
- Freelancer- This one has been around for a while and is a nice backup if the first two don't cut it.

Starting a Startup

This topic has had book after book written on how you would want to go about it. I will pull some knowledge and briefly go over how you might want to go about this.

Model

"The Lean Startup" by Eric Ries is one of the staples of Silicon Valley startup methodology. There is an excellent canvas that you can fill out to help you frame your company you can find on Leanstack.com.

Observe, Prototype and Ask Questions

Before you dive into prototyping I would suggest doing market research and the best kind of market research is seeing if people will buy the damn thing by observing them. Notice how I used the term observing because people often pitch potential customers then ask if they want it. If someone was pitching you hard with a hopeful look in their eyes and you didn't care for the product what would you say? Probably, "Yeah, that's cool" just to get your pesky friend off of your case.

Ask your friends question that are around your product without pitching it, figure out how they use it. Then once you have built it go back to the ones would you thought might use it and ask them questions about it.

For more beyond this step. I suggest reading these books (there are a million more):

- The Mom Test by Rob Fitzpatrick
- The Lean Startup by Eric Ries
- Rework by Jason Fried
- The Hard Thing About Hard Things by Ben Horowitz

Finding A Home

Hopefully now you have a job or startup or freelance job to sustain yourself in Silicon Valley, now you need a place to sleep. As you may have heard housing is very expensive and hard to find in the Bay Area. So get going!

Good Ole' Craigslist

Let's be honest, most every living space anyone has ever found has been on Craigslist. That has been the case with myself besides staying with family. So there are a couple tricks or "hacks" for finding a good place to live using Craigslist.

Hack #1

Create a post that is honest, has a picture and describes that you have recently gotten interested in the Silicon Valley dream and are looking to live with nice interesting people and give the specifications you want. Then post it in all the "neighborhoods" of the city you're trying to move to, varying the message slightly each time. I did this and had over a dozen people emailing me in the city of San Jose.

Hack #2

Get an RSS feed of houses you want to find get sent straight to your phone via text. If you google "What are some good hacks for renting an apartment in San Francisco?" a great Quora article will pop up with tips and tricks.

Due Diligence

Be prepared. The competition for housing is very high so you have to be on time, have all the paper filled out and cash in hand ready to buy. You have to be ready and willing to jump on an opportunity quickly with as much prepared as you can manage.

Negotiate

I was able to negotiate so well that my landlord actually gave me back $300 a few weeks after I had given it to her. Show them you are a good person (hopefully you are) and be honest about your passion to live in Silicon Valley.

Chapter 4
Building A Reputation

You're here! You've made it! You're (hypothetically) living your dream life by living and working in Silicon Valley, what more do you need?!? Well, life can always improve and you need to make sure you are valuable enough to stick around. Many people over the years in Silicon Valley were able to build a reputation off of various tactics and use that to get a job, investment, sell products and a loads of other great things. There are many great ways of doing this, it is much more of a long play as opposed to much of the other strategies in this book.

Blog

Honestly, a well written blog is the most respected way to build a reputation over a long period of time with a huge audience of people. Writing has made a resurgence recently with the popularity platforms like Medium. Finding a specific topic and writing on it for a long period of time is an amazing way to gain a following and mostly gain credibility. However, do not expect to have it blow up or have money pouring into your pockets in a few months. I would say a reasonable time to wait is **2 years** with at least a post a week. That's no ads, cheesy affiliate sales or obvious paid promotion or any other bullshit for that matter. Just solid content that you yourself would have found valuable if it was written by somebody else. Make sure you get a domain, maybe yourname.com or some witty thing you come up with .com. Whatever it is just get it up, if you can't code your own site just use SquareSpace or something like that to have something up.

I use this strategy with my blog youngandfoolish.co (hint), I want to put out really useful content for years with no expectation of any return at all and then do something with it. Try and collect emails by incentivizing people to sign up. My strategy for johnfrye.co (hint hint) and youngandfoolish.co (I think you get it) is to collect emails by giving away this very book for free to all who sign up. So think of all the great things you could do to get sign ups from your lovely followers. Also, if you have not picked up on my subtle hints I would love for you to read and subscribe to youngandfoolish.co, my goal is to help you more then you are helping me by following it!

Social Media

Again, this could be a great way to build a reputation for yourself. Having someone look up your social media and seeing that you have a huge following with lots of engagement will get people over the barrier and start trusting your reputation. This takes time as well, but you can pay for it with ads and promotions. I would not advise that, I would find what content works by testing for months then sticking to that content and posting consistently for years.

Speaking

It may seem to a person starting off like speaking means you've made it, are legitimate and that you have everything figured out. Finding speaking gigs isn't that hard actually and you don't have to have decades of experience.

Starting off offering to speak at small meetups is a great way to start. Colleges have them, there are many on meetup.com and there are small events going on fairly frequently. Find bigger events and just pitch yourself to them, find ones that pay and offer to do it for free or at the very end of another speaker. Have reasons why you'll add value to their crowd and why they'll love you, it's hard to say no to that.

Again, just keep doing this and people will notice you more and more and getting speaker gigs will be easier and much bigger than before. You may even be able to start charging after a few years and launch things off of your personal brand. Be careful though, many people realize that they can get many speaking gigs and over do it. They begin to neglect their business or main income source and that could suffer as a result.

Books

Almost all of the Silicon Valley/Entrepreneurial greats have their own books. Mark Cuban, Sheryl Sandberg, Ben Horowitz, Bill Draper, Paul Graham, Jason Fried, Sophia Amoruso, Gary Vaynerchuck, Seth Godin, Guy Kawasaki, need I go on? I would suggest writing book after you have built a reputation with one of the strategies above. You would want to have it do well based on the following you would have created for yourself.

Conclusion

Thank You!

Thank you so much for reading this, I really hope it was able to guide you on your journey to living your dream life in Silicon Valley. If you want to give feedback, ask questions or just chat feel free to email me at john@johnfrye.co.